I0824474

MOM'S BOOK OF WISDOM

TIMELESS ADVICE
FROM MY MOTHER & YOURS

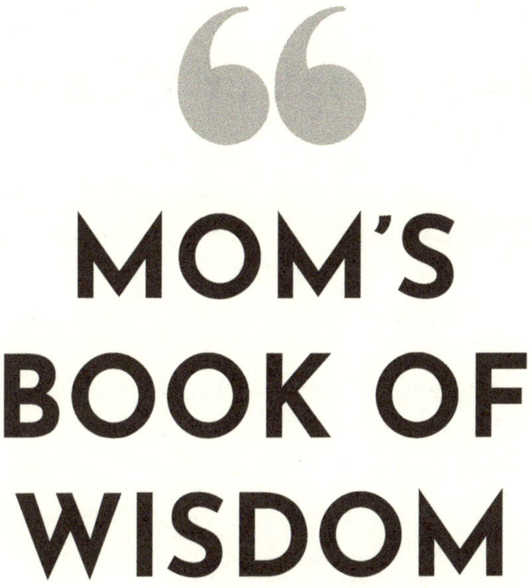

MOM'S BOOK OF WISDOM

NORAH LAWLOR

Hatherleigh Press, Ltd.
62545 State Highway 10, Hobart, NY 13788, USA
hatherleighpress.com

Mom's Book of Wisdom

Library of Congress Cataloging-in-Publication Data
is available.
ISBN: 978-1-57826-841-2

Interior design by Carolyn Kasper
Cover design and edits by Richard Spencer, with
additional edits by Elizabeth Taylor
Printed in the United States

The authorized representative in the EU for
product safety and compliance is Catarina Astrom,
Blästorpsvägen 14, 276 35 Borrby, Sweden.
info@hatherleighpress.com

10 9 8 7 6 5 4 3 2 1

For my mother, Doris Lilian Lawlor, who gave me the inspiration, love, faith, advice, courage and strength to handle life and its challenges.

Contents

Introduction

THE UNIVERSAL LANGUAGE of love, poetically, is ignited by the very person who showered you in that unconditional emotion since the start of your life. From the very first compassionate moment she held you in her arms, your life began—and so did an eternal bond.

Her generosity and empathy made her your first role model. She led you down a path of discovery and formed you into the person you are today. The undeniable impact of mothers, those powerful figures, echoes across time and space—a uniquely human experience that is thankfully shared by billions across the world.

This book is dedicated to the woman in your life who inspired you. The one who motivated you. When a mother's voice speaks, it shares the wisest words. Mothers are the beacons of hope whose message of empowerment is as deep and enduring as their love.

In these pages, I share with you profound words from my own mother, as well as collected thoughts and stories from famous names to personal friends—all of us formed and shaped by the lessons our mothers taught us.

The mother and child bond is celebrated through important lessons, undeniable truths and humor. By collectively sharing our Mother's wisdom, we forever sustain that precious cycle of life.

Each entry is uniquely beautiful and meant to bring you joy as you reflect on the inimitable relationship you have with the most wonderful woman in the world.

1

The Early Years

She simply loved you from the moment she held you in her arms. The beacon of light you saw when you entered the world was the twinkle in her eyes. It was the first time you experienced hope. It was the moment that you understood wisdom. You were born from her love, as she eagerly waited to wrap you in her warm embrace.

It didn't even need to be said, but she told you with all this with that first loving gaze.

That strong mother doesn't tell her cub, "Son, stay weak so the wolves can get you." She says, "Toughen up, this is reality we are living in."

—LAURYN HILL

There is no force equal to a woman determined to rise.

—W. E. B. DU BOIS

The greatest gift a parent can give a child is to love themselves. This is the key to self-empowerment. From there, anything is possible.

—Stacey Cooper, friend

Let choice whisper in your ear and love murmur in your heart. Be ready. Here comes life.

—MAYA ANGELOU

Scratching my head hard, I cannot recall a single piece of direct advice from my mother whilst I was a child. There was plenty when I got older. What I learned from her at that age seems to have been by inference. Perhaps the most salient guidance came at the age of six. There I stood, looking up at her, quaking, having been found out for some transgression or other.

I remember asking, "Mommy, how did you know that I was lying?"

"Well, when you lie, you always raise your eyebrows," she responded.

I spent the next few years of my childhood doing my darndest to keep my eyebrows down. Those furrowed brows must have been like a flashing neon sign until I worked out what was going on. I realized that honesty was the best policy.

To this day, there is nothing by which I set greater store—even though it is sometimes more self-defeating than integrity.

—Stuart MacDonald, friend

Growing up happens in a heartbeat. One day you're in diapers; the next day you're gone. But the memories of childhood stay with you for the long haul.

—KEVIN ARNOLD,

The Wonder Years

While we try to teach our children all about life, our children teach us what life is all about.

—ANGELA SCHWINDT

A mother who radiates self-love and self-acceptance actually vaccinates her daughter against low self-esteem.

—NAOMI WOLF

My Yiddish Gramma, Dora, shared the best lesson on the importance of having a realistic perspective on the relative importance of situations. Whenever my brother or I would complain about something like having to do homework, dinner with no dessert, bedtime, limited TV, she would say, "This should be the worst thing that ever happens to you."

I hated hearing it then, but I value the undeniable wisdom now. How right she was!

—Donna Henes, acquaintance

Cleaning your house while your kids are still growing up is like shoveling the walk before it stops snowing.

—PHYLLIS DILLER

When a child is born the mother also is born again.

—GILBERT PARKER,
Parables of a Province

I love my mother as trees loves water and sunshine. She helps me grow, prosper, and reach great heights.

—TERRI GUILLEMETS

When I was a child, I would occasionally have sleepovers at my cousins' house. They lived on a farm in the country. Before leaving, my mother, Leona O'Hare would always remind me to help my aunt with the household chores and not just spend the whole time playing with my cousins.

She would tell me that my aunt was a busy person, and I was one more body she had to feed and take care of. "So, you had better thank her and show your appreciation by helping her out or she may not let you go there again," my mother would say.

I think doing what she said helped me to recognize and acknowledge what others do for me and that I should always verbally thank them. In addition, I was unaware at the time, but by doing various tasks I was learning experientially.

Another thing I learned from this is that there could be consequences if you don't show your appreciation. I believe that my mother's advice would still hold true today for children, especially for some who are privileged or feel a sense of entitlement.

—Doreen Corriveau, friend

I think she is growing up, and so begins to dream dreams, and have hopes and fears and fidgets, without knowing why or being able to explain them.

—LOUISA MAY ALCOTT

The mother's heart is the child's schoolroom.

—HENRY WARD BEECHER

A mother's example sketches the outline of her child's character.

—TIM HOWARD

My mom was and still is the ultimate baker. You name it, she could make it—from bagels, croissants, sour dough bread, Black Forest cake, to ice cream rolls and the pièce de résistance, her apple tarte tatin, which is as fine a slice as served at Leydoyen in Paris. Decadent and delicious as one would expect.

My childhood and teen years were spent sitting around the kitchen table watching my mother roll, dice, sprinkle, sift, measure, and frost with love. She took great pleasure in sharing her delectable treats. She was always thinking of the next batter, the next cake, the next pie.

My sister and I dreamed of cream puffs, Napoleons, eclairs—no dessert was too challenging for our mom. If we suggested something or had tasted a goody when we were out, she was able to duplicate and make it even better because it was made with love.

One time, a three-layer chocolate cake was cooling on the table and our cat jumped up and dug in. Without a moment's hesitation, mom made a new mix and the situation was salvaged before guests arrived.

This is not about the stories she shared or the words she spoke to us during our time in the kitchen. It is about the love and devotion she poured into her preparations and the chance to spend valuable time with her while she was doing something that she enjoyed. It brought great pleasure to her loved ones. In retrospect, my mom taught me how to share a lick of a spoon, run the mixer, and check the cupcakes with a toothpick.

Feeling proud of your accomplishments is so important—no matter what it is, you are doing it with pride. She taught me how to include others while tackling all types of projects, how to teach, how to give and how sometimes the simple things in life are truly the most important.

I will forever be that young girl sitting at the kitchen table filled with wax paper and dough where I was never afraid of a challenge.

—Adrienne Stern, casting director

Sometimes you will never know the value of a moment until it becomes a memory.

—DR SEUSS

Mothers and their children are in a category all their own. There's no bond so strong in the entire world. No love so instantaneous and forgiving.

—GAIL TSUKIYAMA

My mom has always taught me that knowledge is power and the more I read, the more interesting I will be in any setting.

—Gavin Kelly, entrepreneur

My mother is my root, my foundation. She planted the seed that I base my life on, and that is the belief that the ability to achieve starts in your mind.

—MICHAEL JORDAN

Birth takes a woman's deepest fears about herself and show her that she is stronger than them.

—UNKNOWN

2

Adolescence

The years we spend as teenagers are ones of bliss and anxiety in equal measure. Still too young to fully understand, but too old to not begin to wonder. Innocent elementary classroom days are left behind as we pass through the hallowed doors of high school. We begin to realize that growing up can be hard to do—very hard to do.

These are the years when your mother's wisdom will be full of tough love. She will be kind, but she will also be honest as she shares fundamental life lessons that you will carry for a lifetime.

My mother was my role model before I even knew what that word was.

—LISA LESLIE

My mother, Johnnie Mae, could not read or write, yet I watched her try to write her name in our family Bible every day of her life. We never had a newspaper in our home. This was a time in America when black Americans were not required to attend school, nor vote. They were not Americans; they were slaves…or at least their parents were.

The one thing I ever heard her my mother say about the future was that her children could be able to get an education, even go to college. I made her dream come true by attending NYU—I graduated and got my Associate Degree in 2001—but this was after my mom died.

My mother was a sweet soul. She was never angry, even when there was a reason to be so. Her eyes were so clear, I am sure she was an angel born Black and poor. Other humans may have had education and were so much smarter, but my mother Johnnie Mae had wisdom, intuitiveness, and so much more inner knowledge. I am sure she was God's answer to the truth. I am so thankful that Johnnie Mae was my mother.

—Mary Wilson, The Supremes

A child's life is like a piece of paper on which every person leaves a mark.

—CHINESE PROVERB

A mother is not a person to lean on but a person to make leaning unnecessary.

—DOROTHY C. FISHER

My mother taught me to never gossip. She said it was more a reflection on the person who does the gossiping. It showed their bad manners and insecurities. In the home I grew up in, there was no gossip. Mom was an elegant and loving woman. I have followed her advice. My daughters were raised not to gossip. They were also taught to avoid those who gossip. I do the same.

—Jean Shafiroff, philanthropist

If a man has been his mother's undisputed darling, he retains throughout life the triumphant feeling, the confidence in success, which not seldom brings actual success along with it.

—SIGMUND FREUD

Never judge a person. There are always two sides to the story.

—Jennifer Creel, jewelry designer

Men are what their mothers made them.

—RALPH WALDO EMERSON

My mother's words of wisdom since I was a little girl were to always give in all situations and never expect anything in return. You will always get great joy from giving rather than receiving.

—Suzanne Stepan Coleman, acquaintance

Remember, the goal is not to raise great kids; it's to raise kids who become great adults.

—ANDY ANDREWS

My mother used to tell me, "If you are in a place or with a group of people and feel like you are standing on the ledge of a window, then it's time to go home."

—Pascale Verly, friend

All that I am or ever hope to be, I owe to my angel Mother.

—ABRAHAM LINCOLN

My mother is an extraordinary woman. Her three rules were: First, you can never have a second first impression, so always look your best. But be in a natural way. No need to overdo it either! Second, always be very polite. Manners goes a long way. Then, third, use your charm whenever necessary. Never care about what other people think or say. Be strong and always thank your lucky stars.

—Coralie Paul, Creative Director at CHARRIOL

I learned from my mother that there is a greatness in all of us, and that all of us are delivered to this world with a mission.

—LES BROWN

Act like a lady even if it kills you. The best advice my mother ever gave.

—Jane Pontarelli, realtor

The art of mothering is to teach the art of living to children.

—ELAINE HEFFNER

My mom always said to me, "There is more to life than going to a party."

—Fiona Salmon, friend

My mom has made it possible for me to be who I am. Our family is everything. Her greatest skill was encouraging me to find my own person and own independence.

—CHARLIZE THERON

If you don't ask, the answer is no.

—Katherine Andreassen, actress

All I am, I owe to my mother. I attribute all my success in life to the moral, intellectual and physical education I received from her.

—GEORGE WASHINGTON

One of the best concise messages of advice my mother gave me was when I was about 16 years old and was fretting over whether I was overdressed for a party. She looked at me blankly without giving any credence to my exaggerated complaints and worries and just said, "Whatever you wear, wear it with confidence."

She then walked away and left me, allowing that to sink in and slowly wash away my waves of self-doubt. This simple sentence alluded directly to the idea that one can never be overdressed or underdressed if they own it and are fully confident in their skin as that is the most admirable quality. As I grew, I learned it can also be extended to a larger way of living. It was a lesson to always be unapologetically oneself, as well as to always be proud, confident and comfortable in your skin and with who you are, as that is the greatest tool that equips you for success in all facets of life.

Whether it is simply at a party, in the workplace, at a job interview, on a date, or navigating the nuances of all relationships—both personal and professional—that sentence embodies a mentality that cultivates strength and happiness.

—Avanti Gupta, influencer

Education commences at the mother's knee, and every word spoken within hearsay of little children tends toward the formation of character.

—HOSEA BALLOU

She maintained usually what she enjoyed, like playing tennis and fishing. One needed to have those skills oneself as well as an appreciation of classical music, painting, and drawing. Also, she taught to be charming even though one felt not in the least like it and be able to entertain. Hence one's schooling was important, even if that meant boarding.

I really appreciate that the sentiments were only there because of her love and need to protect. We went through the bombing during World War II with little food and nothing much, but one never felt the least deprived. Our parents were so brave and always made the best of everything no matter what. They always had time for joy and friends.

I am sure that I owe my considerable fortitude to a very strict and disciplined upbringing. It has served me well through tricky times and three children of my own. So, I do have my mother to thank for this even though she was in absentia a lot of the time.

—Vanessa Mitchell, actress

One good mother is worth a hundred schoolmasters.

—GEORGE HERBERT

Of the wealth of advice my mother gave me, this is the piece which I use on almost a daily basis when counseling clients.

It was said to me one cold Saturday morning as my mother was taking me out to practice for my drivers' exam. Growing up in suburban

New Jersey, a driver's license was essential to a teenage social life, without which you were doomed to be at the mercy of your parents to drive you.

I was 16 years old and a bundle of nerves as I drove out my long driveway and headed onto Fairmount Road. My mother, ever perceptive, could see the tightness in my hands. It was at that point she turned to me and said, "You can do this. Remember she who holds the wheel determines the direction."

She gave me the confidence I needed then. As I went off to college, she would again remind me of this advice if I felt scared or overwhelmed. When it came to finances, she would often tell me the same sage guidance—not to let others make financial decisions for me. Maintain control.

—Nicole Noonan, Esq., attorney

For the mother is and must be, whether she knows it or not, the greatest, strongest and most lasting teacher her children have.

—HANNAH W. SMITH

She was a wise woman and she always used to say, "Everything in moderation."

—Pamela Morgan, lifestyle expert

It takes courage to grow up and become who you really are.

—E.E. CUMMINGS

A good mother loves fiercely but ultimately brings up her children to thrive without her. They must be the most important thing in her life, but if she is the most important thing in theirs, she has failed.

—ERIN KELLY, *The Burning Air*

A mother is one to whom you hurry when you are troubled.

—EMILY DICKINSON

3

Inspiration

As you become an adult, you become more aware of your surroundings. This is because the fundamental truths you absorbed as a child from the lessons she taught you have begun to set in, to inform and expand your perspective.

Once you have spread your wings and left the nest, the sky in front of you is vast and ever-changing. On some mornings, there are fluffy white clouds that by afternoon turn into dark storms. Navigating through severe weather can be difficult, but so long as you remember her words, there is always a rainbow at the end of day.

It does not matter your age. You may grow tall and eventually grow out grey hair. But no matter what, you will always be her child.

To a child's ear, "mother" is magic in any language.

—ARLENE BENEDICT

Margaret Guiffre Sullivan said, "Life is short. Never let any grass grow under your feet." It is a Sicilian saying to motivate others to be their best. My mom said this to me when I graduated from college and inspired me to be the best I could be.

—Suzanna Keith, friend

To describe my mother would be to write about a hurricane in its perfect power. Or the climbing, falling colors of a rainbow.

—MAYA ANGELOU

One of my favorite quotes of my mother's is, "You never know and you're never ready." I think this applies to so many aspects of life. Whether it is deciding to have children, make a big move, change jobs…it can be applied to big moments in life and even the smaller ones. You never know, you're never ready, but it's always ok to give it all a try.

—Megan Averbuch, founder of Style50

Parents can only give good advice or put them on the right paths, but the final forming of a person's character lies in their own hands.

—ANNE FRANK

My mother's favorite advice was, "What are you waiting for?" She would say this whenever I would share my dreams or desires. She also talked about listening to and trusting your inner voice, as well as taking a leap of faith. Similarly, she believed in trusting the universe. There are no coincidences. Things happen for a reason. The universe puts you in front of a door and it is your choice to knock, barge in, go around to back door, climb in the window, peek in the window or simply walk away.

—Arlene Winnick, friend

Mothers have as powerful an influence over the welfare of future generations as all other causes combined.

—JOHN ABBOTT

She would say, "Nothing is as bad as it seems." Her name was Idabell Varkle and she was a beauty.

—Linda Dresner, fashion retailer

Behind all your stories is always your mother's story, because hers is where yours begin.

—MITCH ALBOM

"TAHAWOWO: Things Always Have A Way Of Working Out."

Indeed, they do. She would put it on a card or in a text during many of the transitions: flat tires, cancelled flights or moves in my life. It was that simple. And as a forever optimist, I credit this simple outlook she shared to contribute to just that. No matter the challenge, no matter the choice, TAHAWOWO.

My momma is Linda C. McGuire, and she has instilled in me a message of a sunny outlook on all. To many more sunny days ahead!

—Whitney McGuire, acquaintance

There is no influence so powerful as that of the mother.

—SARA JOSEPHA HALE

My mom, Nina Blumenfeld, is a font of wisdom with a strong Brooklyn accent. If I called her because I was upset about something someone said, she would say, "Lynn, consider the source." But with her accent, it sounded like "sauce." And I would respond, "Is that Alfredo, Mom?" And we would crack up.

—Lynn Blumenfeld, ad consultant

A mother is a reservoir of positivity and encouragement.

—SONALI PATHAK

I have always taught my children the simple phrase of, "Give to get." I made it up, but it is my life's mantra. I preface this with: Don't give in order to receive, just give freely of your experience, your compassion, your time. Don't quantify it, but the great wheel of life turns and those who give abundantly with an open pure heart will find many blessings coming their way.

—Clo Cohen, Creative Director of T. Anthony

The influence of a mother upon the lives of her children cannot be measured. They know and absorb her example and attitudes when it comes to questions of honesty, temperance, kindness, and industry.

—BILLY GRAHAM

Once I said something that I thought at the time was extremely rude and disrespectful to my mother. I went to apologize saying, "You're my mother and it showed no respect to say that."

"I'm not interested in that kind of respect," she told me. "I want you to respect what I read and the poetry I love. Why I love your father so much, why we are in the business that we are in, what that struggle is…why we persevere." She said that is what I want you to respect me for as a woman.

That was quite a lesson.

—Brenda Vaccaro, actress

Behind every young child who believes in himself is a parent who believed first.

—MATTHEW L. JACOBSON

I can think of my second mother who always told me, "I can't afford to buy cheap things."

—Fiona Salmon, friend

Moms are as relentless as the tides. They just don't drive us to practice, they drive us to greatness.

—STEVE RUSHIN

When my friend Sue's mother was dying, and she knew it, she reassured her daughter and said, "Dying isn't so bad." It gave her daughter comfort.

—Richard Spencer, writer & editor

My mother is a poem I'll never be able to write, though everything I write is a poem to my mother.

—SHARON DOUBIAGO

My mother's advice takes on more meaning every day. Her name was Pearl Weiner and she said, "Things that we worry about before they happen often are never as bad as we fear, so there is no use stressing ahead of time."

—Sue Weiner, writer

A mother is a woman who shows you the light when you just see the dark.

—GRIMALDOS ROBIN

When things get difficult, I always remember my grandmother Liisa. She lived on the Estonian island of Hiiumaa, near Sweden, in the middle of the Baltic Sea. Liisa was a young woman during WWII, with three young daughters and a sick husband. One day, her house was bombed and burned down, and her youngest daughter and husband were killed.

My mother, who was the middle child, told me that as they were watching the house and everything they owned hopelessly burn in the fire, my grandmother took her and her older sister's hand and said, "At least we have our health and each other."

Eventually, she rebuilt her house toward the end of the war and lived in it during the Soviet time until she died at age 94. When I think of her, I know that I can get through anything.

—Eha Urbsalu, actress

4

Relationships

The quality time you spend with your mother is even more precious as you grow up and become an adult. The years that pass and the lessons you have learned educate you about everything in life, including the relationships you form outside of the immediate family.

Even here, your mother is your teacher. She was your first role model, your standard for unconditional love. She showed you, in both word and deed, what it means to truly care about someone and act accordingly.

The one constant, faithful, inviolable, holy love of loves—the love of your life—is not your wife or lover, it is your mother.

—SANDRA CISNEROS

My mom said, "Marry your best friend. You may have money problems or sex problems, but they will still be your best friend." Love, laughter and happiness."

—Kim Freehill, friend

My mother gave me pearls of wisdom every day, and which I use every day. One of my favorites is, "Be nice to your neighbors. No matter what you have been through, no matter how irritating, no matter how much their belief or politics differ from yours, be nice to them. Your house may be on fire one day, and you'll want them to throw a bucket of water on it."

Mary Frances Powell, my mom, grew up with nothing fancy on a farm in Oklahoma but lacked for nothing. She was a military wife during World War II; raised five kids on a shoestring but made us feel richer than the doctors' kids. She ran the family business alongside my dad, working at least as hard if not harder. And she survived breast cancer at age 90 only to be taken by colon cancer and a massive stroke two years later. We are convinced the stroke was her way of getting out of the whole mess.

We had amazing fun together, from doing crafts as far back as I can remember, to showing her around New York City at Thanksgiving for her 90th birthday. She charmed everyone, even getting us to the front row of the Macy's parade. She is so much a part of me forever.

—Andrea Powell, actress

The most important thing a father can do for his children is to love their mother.

—THEODORE HESBURGH

In my early 20s after a particularly unwanted breakup with a cad of a guy, my mother shared with me advice she had received from her mother, who had received the same advice from her mother. It goes, “If a man would ever leave you, speed him on his way!”

It is advice I learned to follow that led me to my beloved husband of 29 years.

Another momism is, “Nothing is worth a wrinkle.”

—Deborah Dixon, friend

When my children were young, my husband and I worked half days, 12 hours per day. We are self-employed. My mom always said money is cold. You cannot hug it and it certainly will not hug you back. So, learn to balance your time. Spend time with your husband, kids, family, and friends.

Other things Mom would always say is you can't put an old head on young shoulders, as well as you can't teach an old dog new tricks.

Mom always would say the secret to a long and happy marriage is respect each other and communicate.

—Rosanne Isom, friend

No human mother was ever designed to be the sole source of sustaining life energy for her child without also receiving outside support for herself and her own individual needs.

—CHRISTIANE NORTHRUP

My mother, Lea Shabat, born in Morocco to Jewish parents, immigrated to Canada in the 60s where my brother and I were born and raised. Every Friday, without fail, she would prepare a Shabbat dinner. Whether it was just the four of us or 20 guests, she always made several courses for her family recipes. From couscous with lamb, to chicken with saffron and meatballs with celery and peas, she never managed to break into a sweat.

The house had that special Shabbat smell every week and before she served us, she would go upstairs to shower, wash her hair, paint her nails red, put on her caftan and come down as the queen of her household, which she was.

Her best lesson to me was to learn how to be a good cook because if you do, you will always have people around your table. To this day, it is true and swear by it. Hosting people around my table is one of my favorite things to do.

—Stephanie Manasseh, art curator

Sending a handwritten note is one of the thoughtful practices my mother taught me as a child. She emphasized the importance of letting people know your appreciation and acknowledgement of them, whether it is for their love, a loss in their life, a celebratory moment, a sickness they may be facing, or a gift they have bestowed upon you.

She made writing notes fun, which started with pulling out colorful markers or finding wildflowers to press for our own cards. Surprisingly, when you pass along a kind gesture with a signature touch of your own, it is a gift that goes both ways—from the sender and to the recipient.

This holiday season I received a beautiful box of Cartier notepaper with my name on it and was immediately reminded of my mother and our card-making creations. I could not wait to put my pen to the paper and let my friends and family out there know how much I miss seeing them. Of course, I will send a note to my mother as well letting her know how much I love her.

—Kristen Ingersoll, fashion director

A man loves his sweetheart the most, his wife the best, but his mother the longest.

—IRISH PROVERB

Growing up in Australia in the 40s and 50s was vastly different to the world today, although I continue to remind myself of my mother's remarks.

Friday night was cinema night, usually some silly romantic Hollywood classic or musical, as my mother was a dreamer and her daily life differed greatly from the movies. They were her escape. One evening as we sat and waited for my father to come home and I asked her, "Why did you marry Dad?" I asked if it was because he was romantic or handsome. She looked at me and laughed, something she seldom did.

My mother replied it was to escape Nana (her mother) as she was the middle child of eleven children, which made her life very difficult. As we continued talking, she became profoundly serious and told me to never get married.

"Why?" I asked. "Doesn't everyone get married?" Her response was that marriage is a trap, a waiting game. She said you wait for the men to come back from the war, you wait for them to come home from work, the pub, the races, the football and hanging out with their mates. You wait for your kids to be born, wait for them to grow up, wait for them to leave you, and then wait and hope for them to come and pay a visit.

She told me, "When you grow up, go to America and find your dream. Move to America and become a movie star, a dancer and be happy."

I did not become a movie star, nor a dancer or a singer, but I did move to America at 21 and I did find myself. Not as her dream, but as my own. I became a fashion designer and later opened a prestigious art gallery in New York City. Years later, during her trips to New York, I would take her to Broadway musicals and as she sat eagerly on the edge of her seat, I could see she was up there, living her dream.

In the end, I did not listen to her advice. I just celebrated my 58th wedding anniversary.

—Maureen Zarember, art gallery director

A mother's love and wisdom empower our children to flourish, instilling in them the courage to reach their full potential.

—MELANIA TRUMP

My mother was my best friend and my acting manager. She was the coolest chick I have ever known. She had pink hair before it was in fashion, as well as only wearing one dangly earring. She was an art teacher for the board of education as well as a commissioned muralist.

Her life motto was, "Stop giving a shit." She taught me to unapologetically be myself in whatever situation life may bring. She taught me to not fear judgment. She taught me to never sweat the small stuff.

My mother Mindy Waks had her life taken by glioblastoma multiform stage 4 brain cancer out of nowhere. Since that day, when minor problems arise, I can see myself shrugging it off as she taught me.

—Aesha Waks, friend

My mother always said not to talk too much. Listen and you'll learn new things.

—Marie-Claire Gladstone, realtor

5

Career & Finances

As much as you would like to be a kid forever, eventually we all grow up. We cannot all be Peter Pan. With age comes responsibility, as your mother was likely the very first to point out in your life.

She taught you that the transition from school days to workdays is not always fun, but a necessity for becoming a real adult. How you spend your first years completely on your own is a testament to the wisdom she shared with you on how to do everything from saving money to conducting business meetings.

Your mother was your first financial advisor, as well as your first boss. How she found time to do it all is just one of those great mysteries of life.

Never work just for money or for power. They won't help save your soul or help you sleep at night.

—MARIAN WRIGHT EDELMAN

Be anything you want to be.

—Claire Khodara, singer

My mother Clemencia Rolon is the person who has taught me about embracing change and having a willingness to pivot and adapt to the change. She migrated from Paraguay to the U.S. by way of Mexico and with the guidance of a coyote.

When she came over, she was a math teacher. By the time she got here with no understanding of the language and no teaching license, she became a housekeeper. Once she learned the language she made her way into very prestigious kitchens and became a chef. From there she decided to go to school and get a degree in the U.S.

She then opened a store front and did custom window treatments, interior design and home decor. Most recently, she opened a party rental supply in South America. All her businesses were successful in their own ways. Whenever a shift presented itself, she made the respective shifts needed to adapt to the change. With fewer words on the matter but a massive call to action, she has taught me to appreciate the way change forces us to adapt.

—Manny Rolon, friend

My mother's lesson that no matter what you do, always be the best at what you do. Even if you are a garbage collector, be the best garbage collector you can be. I became me with this guidepost.

—Randy Lampert, friend

"My mother always said an Oscar nomination couldn't hurt."

—Roger Friedman, publisher, Showbiz411

You can only become truly accomplished at something you love. Don't make money your goal. Instead, pursue the things you love doing, and then do them so well that people can't take their eyes off you.

—MAYA ANGELOU

My mother Barbara Alexis told me, "Bring your work closer to you." If I am in the kitchen, I repeat that phrase as I am cutting, cooking or scooping something up. When I notice that my bowl or pan is too far away, I slide the farthest item closer to me so I don't make a mess. I find things work much better and are way less messy when I bring all my items closer to me.

—Kim Alexis, actress and model

First quote that comes to mind is, "You can do anything you want as long as you can afford it." This is a quote that came at me often in regard to apartments I rented, clothes I wanted to buy or trips I wanted to take. Second was, "Stay out of the fast lane." This, of course, was in regard to dating.

—Laura Lysle, friend

Mother love is the fuel that enables a normal human being to do the impossible.

—MARION C. GARRETTY

I grew up in a close-knit family in the Midwest where, when you graduated college, you moved back to live next door. But upon graduation, my mother told me that I needed to go to New York and follow my creative passions as there was no place for me in Ohio.

It was a great personal sacrifice that I only fully understand now that I too have a young daughter. Thus, here is the quote in this context, "Being born in the Midwest does not define you or your future."

It was just a fact. Your life will be what you make of it and you need to push out of your comfort zone to attain what you are destined to be. My mother is Renee Demsey.

—John Demsey, former Executive Group President at Estée Lauder Companies

I think every working mom probably feels the same thing: You go through big chunks of time where you're just thinking, 'This is impossible—oh, this is impossible.' And then you just keep going and keep going, and you sort of do the impossible.

—TINA FEY

It was 1979 when I left Ottawa to live in Vancouver. I was 19 and had no plan for my future. When I left, I broke my mother's heart. I was her only daughter and the baby after six boys.

I stayed for three years, then returned to Ottawa after receiving numerous letters and calls from mom. I didn't know what to do with my life and she gave me the direction I needed.

She had been modeling for many years in Ottawa and one of her model friends opened a makeup school. She said I had to find something I loved doing and had passion for. That is why at 23 I went to makeup school and became a professional makeup artist. I owe my life to my mom. Now I'm taking care of her in her senior years.

—Susan Kealey, make-up artist

Being a mother has been the most challenging and the most rewarding position I will ever hold.

—CATHY SHAFFER

My mother Eunice Jane Conley was born March 29, 1919, to Sarah Jane Conley and George Conley in Montreal. She was the middle child of seven children.

Growing up through The Great Depression and World War II, there were hard times. She helped her mother in the home with the other siblings and was always willing to jump in to assist in baking, cooking and cleaning. She did work at part-time jobs in retail stores to help with making money. She had a beautifully gifted voice and took singing lessons to enhance her talent.

In 1938, she started singing in various churches and summer camps and was paid a very minimal wage. She had a gift from God to sing. This is where she met my father. He saw her singing at church and through other friends they were introduced.

The war separated them for a long time. He was a draftsman and builder and stayed an extra year after the war to rebuild bridges and buildings. Upon his return to Montreal, he married my mother.

They lived in Montreal for one year then moved to Ottawa so he could open his own business. He bought land and designed and built homes. My mother's journey was only just beginning. She was an at-home mom raising four kids under the age of seven. She was busy—a Martha Stewart of her time, always baking, cooking, entertaining, especially friends from our church. Her faith, her loyalty to her church and her love for her family made it seem so easy.

But her journey was hard. By 1967, Dad's business was in trouble. My mother was industrious, creative and on point—very driven, no time to sit down or relax. She was always creating ways to make money to help with the expenses of the household.

She worked hard in her community, always sewing for ladies in the church and her neighborhood. She started to sell Singer sewing machines and then started to teach women how to sew by creating sewing classes. Then she went to the Ottawa school board to suggest they have sewing classes in their program for night classes, which she then started up herself.

This was truly an inspiration to us all. Entrepreneurship was there, and we witnessed it with my mom all through her life. She had many jobs in her life, mostly working with her hands. Life's lessons were shown by example.

In the Bible, Proverbs 31:31 says, "Honor her for all that her hands have done, and let her works bring her praise at the city gate." My mother sadly passed away December 2019 at 100 years old. My mother believed in me. She was my rock.

In 1992, I started up my own clothing business, which was my dream for many years. My mother worked for me doing alterations from 1993 to 2009. She loved being involved with my clients and was a major asset to my business. She had a career of sewing, dressmaking and alterations in the Ottawa community which spanned over 60 years.

This dedication to her craft inspired me and was a blueprint for my entrepreneurship, as well as my choice to endeavor in the fashion industry. I believe I was shown life's lessons by example. My mother was an elegant and strong, independent woman. I feel blessed to have had the opportunity to know her more closely during the last few years. She is missed, but I feel her close to me in my heart.

—Earlene Hobin, friend

A housewife deserves to be honored as much as a woman who earns her living in the marketplace. I consider bringing up children a responsible job. In fact, being a good housewife seems to me a much tougher job than going to the office and getting paid for it.

—BETTY FORD

Although not college educated, my mother was a very smart woman. She encouraged me to have piano lessons, advising that it would always be something you have for a great enjoyment. My father was a professional piano player. As much as I tried, I really never got a grip on playing piano. I regret it to this day.

My mother always impressed upon me to learn Spanish, as that would be the language of the future in California. Following her advice, I enrolled in Spanish at UCLA. Unfortunately, I was the only non-speaking Hispanic in the classroom and my first grade was an F.

When deciding on a major, my mother encouraged me to be a dentist, stating (correctly) that there would always be a need for dentists. Unfortunately, I didn't have the manual dexterity necessary and in pursuing a pre-dental major was unable to cut a piece of chalk into a tooth. By process of elimination, I became a lawyer.

My mother taught me compassion, understanding, and work ethic simply by watching her.

Most importantly, she emphasized the importance of moderation and health. She stressed eating organic food, not drinking, and not smoking. My mother's name is Mary Shapiro.

—Robert Shapiro, attorney

When I was a child, my mother said to me, "If you become a soldier, you'll be a general. If you become a monk, you'll end up as the pope." Instead, I became a painter and wound up as Picasso.

—PABLO PICASSO

My grandmother Isabel Norton, a professor of linguistics and English at Stony Brook University, brought me up from the age of seven until I was a young teenager.

She said, "Rolise, never read a book about a book until you have read the book. Your opinion is just as valuable as the person who wrote the book about the book and they are not always correct. I correct books all the time."

She had in fact corrected books as I had seen them and now I correct and write in books. I have shelves of them.

Several years ago, Bryan Sykes, the human geneticist at Oxford University and leading geneticist in Great Britain was quoted as not knowing why a blonde, blue-eyed baby was born to a Nigerian couple. I had recently read his book *The Seven Daughters of Eve* and I knew his work, but I had also read *Herodotus, The Histories.* While

Sykes was not wrong, he was not informed; Herodotus clearly states that Hanno, the Phoenician/Canaanite navigator, had circumnavigated Africa and most believe he created an outpost in Cameroon, but they were not certain on its exact location.

Nigeria is next to Cameroon. It is also stated that the Tribe of Dan had red hair and lived in their ships. Many have deduced that they are one and the same people or that they traveled together. It is also stated that the Phoenicians traveled to the Sicily Islands of Great Britain and created an outpost there. In the letter, I let Sykes know that I believed it was recessive genes on both parent's sides from the Phoenicians or those traveling with them. Since then, I've taught myself the Hebrew and Phoenician letters as they are one in the same.

I would never have had the confidence to contact one of the world's leading geneticists had my grandmother not given me the validity to do so. It truly was a gift, as that confidence has opened doors to a world I normally wouldn't believe could be my own. Now, I have phone calls from family members who say, "Where are you?" And if I answer the United Nations, the Ukrainian Embassy, or at a private cocktail party with the Mayor of New York they don't believe me, but they were not given the gift I was by my grandmother.

—Rolise Rachel, influencer

I thought about this for a while because my mother has taught me so much by just watching her. She is an artist by trade. But some of the most profound and important wisdom my mother gave me was to always believe in myself.

She said stand tall and look the person right in the eye when meeting them. She said to say my full name and reach out my hand with a smile, as well as to shake hands. She taught me the importance of confidence and how important first impressions can be. For example, in my interviews when I would go for jobs, such as with the airlines or modeling, this would always lead to at least a callback or nailing the job offer.

A mother can instill so many gifts for life. Confidence is one of them.

—Sarah Johnson, acquaintance

My mother taught me not to care what others think and always be kind. You cannot please everyone, and you only live once so you might as well be your true authentic self.

My mother Bernadette Chaplin was born and grew up Catholic in Northern Ireland in a Protestant area. She grew up having to be tough. I think it made her not care what others thought of her. She would get called names constantly for being Catholic.

When I started modeling, I would sometimes get insecure and she would always tell me, "Fuck the rest. You're the best!" This was said in a strong Irish accent, which would make me laugh. After a giggle I would think, 'She's right! Let's get on with it.'

—Kiera Chaplin, model and actress

I do not think I am successful just because I have money. I'm successful because I love who I am and I have no regrets.

—SUZE ORMAN

My mother raised me to be strong and independent, in life and financially. Because of my mother, I have always had a perfect credit score and never knew how important that was until my later years. Her biggest advice was to never depend on a man. You always need your own money, your own private account and always hope for the best, but plan for the worst.

I am coming out of an extremely hard relationship with a wealthy man who seemed like he was my dream but ended up being my nightmare. I am happy I had this ingrained into me because this relationship could have gone very differently, especially as I built a company from the ground up out of my savings.

I lost pretty much everything due to the pandemic, so when I met him, he seemed to be a gift from God. He was good-looking, treated me like I was the most special woman in the world, and showered me with love and gifts. He tried to sell me on this amazing future filled with love, happiness, and anything I could imagine. He even offered to buy me a boutique in a small town so I wouldn't have to stress about my hospitality and event company. Then he started to show what a lunatic he really is and when he proposed to me with the biggest rock you could ever imagine, I ran.

I am now living with my cousin in Connecticut but could have easily stayed in his mansion in Long Island with him. I could have had my financial future completely set and at the same time lived a miserable life. Overall, my mother saved my life since the break-up.

It is a crazy world out there and my mother was nowhere near perfect but watching her go through what she did with men and her constantly showing me a life I do not want has given me a life I do.

—Jackie Botelho, friend

My mother always said, "Waste not, want not."

—Lori Price, friend

6

Children of Your Own

The circle of life continues with the joy of bearing children for many individuals. Marriage leads to offspring who fill days with tiny footsteps and precious giggles. A baby changes everything, especially the way you view the lessons your mother taught you.

To hold your own baby is a gift. Even those who are aunts and uncles understand the sweetness of an infant and how they influence a deeper level of joy. Your mother knew this fact, which is why she shared her knowledge about parenthood with you.

Her words are often the first thing you hear in your mind when you look deeply into a child's eyes.

Motherhood changes everything.

—ADRIANA TRIGIANI

A mother's happiness is like a beacon, lighting up the future but reflected also on the past in the guise of fond memories.

—HONORÉ DE BALZAC

There comes a time in every mother's life when you no longer know everyone your child does. When they are little, you are the CEO of their life and nothing happens unless you put your stamp of approval on it. But around sixth or seventh grade, new kids come to the school or into their social lives that you don't have the opportunity to meet. All of a sudden, your child is going over to so-and-so's house for a party and you have met neither child nor parent. It was about this time that I got the best piece of parenting advice, not from my mother, but from a wise older mother who had gone through the same thing years before me.

We met while on vacation and discovered we were from the same town and coincidentally, her children had gone to the same school that mine now attended. I was bending her ear about my sudden loss of total control over their lives and she told me something I'll never forget. She said, "Don't settle for not knowing. Make a point of knowing all their friends and watch them very carefully. No matter how great you kids are, they will never survive bad friends." Indeed.

—Laurie Gelman, author

Motherhood has a very humanizing effect. Everything gets reduced to essentials.

—MERYL STREEP

A mother's arms are made of tenderness and children sleep soundly in them.

—VICTOR HUGO

From my wife: "My mother lived by example. She seldom used two words when one would do. When I was 22, I told her that she was a successful parent. I always knew what she would say or do in any situation, whether I chose to follow it or not. Even to this day, this is true."

—David S. Rose, entrepreneur

I believe the choice to become a mother is the choice to become one of the greatest spiritual teachers there is.

—OPRAH WINFREY

Life doesn't come with a manual, it comes with a mother.

—UNKNOWN AUTHOR

My mother Tina Hebert always told me, "You get out of life what you put into it."

She also said, "As long as you're true to yourself and good to others, life will be good to you."

I gave birth naturally to my son. During the delivery my mom, my cousin and bestie were by my side from start to finish. I naturally assumed my mom would be by my side the entire time. Well, she had wife duties to handle at home, so she left and said she'd be back in a little bit. That little bit turned into longer than 24 hours.

So, I had a moment of reflection when I had to go to the restroom and the baby was crying.

I needed help to get out of my bed and someone to watch the baby. Unfortunately, my nurse wasn't available at the moment so I was all alone. So, I picked Greycen up and took him to the restroom with me. For all the mothers out there, you know using the restroom is quite the challenge after giving birth.

I started to cry and then out of nowhere I just looked down at my son and realized that from this point on I have a life that I'm responsible for. I found this inner strength and confidence I never knew I had. I stopped crying and made it work. Even though my mother hasn't missed a moment since, I feel everything happens for a reason because I needed to know that I could do it with no help. That was the moment I knew we'd be just fine.

Greycen is 16 months now and is thriving, healthy, happy and very smart. He can identify the letters in his name, go to the potty, feed himself, pray before he eats his meals and loves story time. My journey as a mother is just beginning, but so far I've been able to apply advice from my amazing mother and a few other mothers I look up to. I have been able to set a solid foundation for my growing boy.

Being a parent is not easy by far, but it is the greatest feeling in the world.

—Willissa Ari Hebert, acquaintance

I feel more beautiful than I've ever felt because I've given birth. I have never felt so connected, never felt like I had such a purpose on this earth.

—BEYONCÉ KNOWLES

My mother's love has always been a sustaining force for our family, and one of my greatest joys is seeing her integrity, her compassion, her intelligence reflected in my daughters.

—MICHELLE OBAMA

I was lucky because my own mother Elizabeth Pulley was a school counselor. She wrote and illustrated a book on parenting called *You Drive the Bus: A Guidebook for Busy Moms.*

I grew up in a small town outside of Cincinnati Ohio, called Mariemont, and I would say her advice was always rooted in those Midwestern values. Namely the big four, those being honesty (tell the truth), consideration for others (think about other people's feelings and not just your own), kindness (treat others the way you want to be treated), and love (make sure your children know they are loved completely and unconditionally).

Favorite expressions included: "This too shall pass," "You never know what's around the corner," "Never give up," and "Keep the faith."

A central theme of her book is that parenting is not easy and it is not for the selfish. When your little birdies have gained the independence and confidence to leave the nest, then that is a job well done.

On another note, my mother also had a fascination with the psychology of relationships, specifically male/female romantic relationships. This has influenced me in the founding of my own company, Pink Wisdom, which offers advice and support from woman to woman.

Lastly, my mother loved to dance. This was in the 1970s and 1980s. I have many memories of waking up and coming downstairs to see her dancing as her early morning exercise in our living room to the sounds of The Supremes, Billy Joel, and—this was a big one—The Emotions' "You've Got the Best of My Love."

I have inherited this trait. I pull up my playlist and get down with a hot dance break nearly every single day.

—Alison Chace, actress

The natural state of motherhood is unselfishness. When you become a mother, you are no longer the center of your own universe. You relinquish that position to your children.

—JESSICA LANGE

Mothers give up so much, so that their children can have so much.

—CATHERINE PULSIFER

My mother was a unique woman. So many things she said and taught me have become part of my DNA as a mother, a businesswoman, a friend and a human being.

When I was a young girl, she made me do house chores such as washing dishes by hand despite the fact we had a dishwasher. Later, she taught me how to clean bathrooms, dust properly, polish silver, clean crystal, iron, clean hairbrushes daily, and hand wash lingerie.

We did closet cleaning every season and donated anything we had not worn or did not like. To this day, I do the same. Luckily, I have daughters, so some of the beautiful things I do not wear go to them or their friends. I still receive letters from my children's friends who felt more confident in that job interview in a simple Valentino suit or a lightly worn pair of Manolo's. Those young people—who I will never know well—still take the time to this day to write or email photos and share how special they felt in a particular cocktail dress I no longer had a need for.

My mother taught me donating clothing to your local church, synagogue, homeless shelter is nothing to take pride in—it's a way to clean your closet without feeling wasteful.

Giving away your old coats and shoes is not considered a mitzvah because it is a cleansing to one's own self. The gift is in the giving and a reminder of, "There by the grace of God."

Acts of sharing things you don't need can help someone in need who you will never meet. She always said, "You never know how life can suddenly change." She was the youngest of seven and her own mother passed away when she was only 13 years old. Her father lost everything in The Great Depression and the siblings had to care for one another and their father.

In life, the more armed you are for anything the more confident you will be. She continued to share, "I hope nothing ever happens in your life that these skillsets are your only option.

The gift is the more you know about the small things in life, the more you will want to know about everything."

My life has certainly taken many twists and turns, but I felt I could manage any situation with confidence should I need to.

In keeping with her credo, she taught me it is important to be kind to everyone but particularly kind to those people who don't receive the gratitude they deserve. Small actions of kindness and generosity not only keep you grounded, they benefit you more in the grand scheme of life. It is an exercise on how to conduct yourself as a human being.

She was an extraordinary woman in many ways, and I miss her dearly every day since her passing in 2012. Everything good about her and what she taught me about life has been passed on to my own children. Her imperfections have also taught me to not be or do certain things.

I am very proud of my three children who are now grown adults. I'm blessed to have had a mother who bothered to teach and share her beliefs. I'm blessed to see the fruits of my mother's labor live on, thereby allowing her to live on within us forever influencing our lives.

—Lori Shabtai, realtor

What greater aspiration and challenge are there for a mother than the hope of raising a great son or daughter?

—ROSE KENNEDY

The only love that I really believe in is a mother's love for her children.

—KARL LAGERFELD

My mother said the cure for thinking too much about yourself was helping somebody who was worse off than you.

—SYLVIA PLATH, *The Bell Jar*

7
Hardships

Life is full of challenges. Not every day is full of sunshine. The days that are stormy and dark are often the ones we need the most advice to get us through.

From trivial messes to big life-changing moments, your mother was always ready to help support you through it all. Her words of wisdom shine through like a beacon of light on our worst days. With love, she steers you to the light at the end of the tunnel with her messages of hope.

I remember my mother's prayers and they have always followed me. They have clung to me all my life.

—ABRAHAM LINCOLN

My mother would say things like don't take your problem with you to the grave. Don't play the victim. It's not so important to always be right. She would also say I don't care how much money anyone has, it's not in my pocket. It's only the expectations that make you unhappy.

—Minnie Osmenia, friend

No one's really doing it perfectly, I just think you love your kids with your whole heart, and you do the best you possibly can.

—REESE WITHERSPOON

When I was nine, my mother Liudmila was diagnosed with cancer and given six months' time to live. My mother was a medical doctor, so she understood what her diagnosis meant. She would not be around to teach me all the things that mothers normally take a lifetime to teach their daughters.

She dedicated every minute of every day she had left to pass to me the things her mother taught her and the lessons and wisdom she had learned on her own.

The cancer diagnosis was the worst news we could have received, but it resulted in an unusually close relationship between a mother and her teenage daughter. My mother's intense commitment made me who I am today.

My mother taught me that as a woman:

1. Be independent and take care of myself.
2. No drama. Life is tough enough already.
3. Be happy and avoid negative energy.
4. The day you get married is the beginning of your courtship, not the end. Work on your relationship and yourself every day.
5. Never stop learning.
6. Always stay interesting.
7. Be adventurous and experience the beautiful, amazing world.

I miss my mother very much, but as I thought about what to write, I realized that she succeeded. I remember what she taught me, where she taught me and the lesson behind each point. Most importantly, I now feel the obligation to do the same for my daughter. In a way, teaching her the things my mother taught me will give her a way to have an attachment to and an understanding of the grandmother she never met, In a way, she will know.

—Inga Kozel, socialite

It's not easy being a mother. If it were easy, fathers would do it.

—DOROTHY ZBORNAK,
The Golden Girls

I lost my father in a tragic accident when I was 18. I have no brothers and my sister had left Milan at the age of 24 for the American dream. My mother is the only relative that I have in in my life. Education, discipline, and integrity were always her top priority. She was a professor of cardiology at the University of Milan. She dedicated all her life after my father passed just for my success.

—Paolo Zampolli, businessman

My instinct is to protect my children from pain. But adversity is often the thing that gives us character and backbone. It's always been a struggle for me to back off and let my children go through difficult experiences.

—NICOLE KIDMAN

When I turned 50, it was the middle of quarantine. I was not depressed, but I wasn't thrilled either. My mom and I were talking, and I told her I was sad, being 50 and single and didn't know where my life was going.

She said simply, "It is a good age. You suddenly know who you are, and you find yourself. And you can keep moving forward. Everything has been better than you feared."

Two years before that, I had to move back to the States after living in the UK for years. I said, "Maybe I was meant to come back. I had been unhappy for a while." She said, "You need a big change and shake-up in your life."

She knew I was afraid but thought it was the best thing for me. She never pushed me before and always wanted me to follow my dreams, but I guess she knew. When she said everything has been better than I feared on my lockdown birthday, she knew what she was saying. Her name is Diane.

—Alyssa Sherman, friend

Successful mothers are not the ones that never struggled. They are the ones that never give up, despite the struggles.

—SHARON JAYNES

I am sure that if the mothers of various nations could meet, there would be no more wars.

—E.M. FORSTER

My mother grew up in an abusive, alcoholic home in the blue-collar suburbs of Philadelphia. Her early life was a horror, but she was brilliant. Her education saved her, and she ended up having a brilliant career in medicine.

She is one of the most positive, curious, intelligent, and hopeful women that I know. She taught me that education is freedom, therapy and self-care are a necessity. There is always room to heal and grow and become who you are meant to be.

—Anne Richardson Hansen, actress & writer

Whenever my mother wanted to keep me grounded, she would tell me to stay in my sneakers.

—Consuelo Vanderbilt Costin, singer,
songwriter & entrepreneur

I remember one thing that stood out especially as we were all struggling with the pandemic in various ways: we were very fortunate not to be suffering, as so many people struggled to keep their lives together.

My mom, Ann Cline, told me that surmounting the feeling of boredom was important in life. Since I was so rarely bored before, I never understood until that year what that meant when I had to create new hobbies during lockdown. I taught myself to play piano and started riding horses.

—Pamela Johananoff, designer

My grandmother Margaret Sylvester use to say, "PNA: Pay No Attention."

—Michelle Russell Johnson, friend

In times of need, and in times of tears, in times of joy and in times of fears...there is mom. The one person who is always there.

—HEATHER STILLUFSEN

"Always leave your place in the world better than when you found it."

I have long said I am the woman. I am because of God, family and country. I am not shy when discussing my faith and love of America, nor do I hesitate in devotion to my mother, Caramine Kellam.

She is my role model. It is she who instilled in me my sense of civic duty and helped form the principles by which I live today. It is from her that I seek advice. Her words are consistent sources of counsel over the years.

My mother has long led by example. Throughout my childhood and education in Virginia, and well into adulthood, Mother and I would often speak about civic duty; she served in leadership roles on several boards and I loved to hear the pride in her voice when she spoke about the AMA Alliance, the AMA-Education and

Research Foundation, the Eastern Shore Community College Foundation, and the Riverside Health Services Foundation.

She would reiterate how important it was to leave one's place better—a lesson well learned from her mother and father, Amine and Polk Kellam.

Today, though Mother has retired from her boards, she still heeds her own advice—her kindness and generosity to those in everyday places, such as the grocery store and doctors' offices, are definitely better because of her.

"Do not confuse dignity and gentility with weakness. Grace under pressure."

Mother served as the first female Chairman of the Hospital Board of Trustees. Her intelligence, charm and strength, as well as ability to manage contrary opinions and quell disagreement with respect and perceived consideration, compelled the trustees to ask her to serve a second term, making her the first person to ever serve twice.

Throughout my career and personal life, these words have been my mantra. There have been a few who mistook our graciousness as weakness. They have not made that mistake twice.

In 2020, Mother was diagnosed with perineal cancer—an incurable cancer that develops in a thin layer of tissue that lines the abdomen. My world imploded, but hers did not. Mom is an exceptional mother and friend; it was during our initial conversation about her cancer that she said, "I have reached the point in life where I don't care what anyone thinks of me but me." Between us, I think she reached this point a long time ago.

Mother is now 80 and her cancer is dormant. I have a feeling she will soon be following the words she once told me: "You don't know what is around the corner, until you turn it." Mom, I can't wait to turn it with you!

—Somers Farkas, U.S. Ambassador to Malta

A mother is the truest friend we have, when trials heavy and sudden fall upon us; when adversity takes the place of prosperity; when friends desert us; when trouble thickens around us, still will she cling to us, and endeavor by her kind precepts and counsels to dissipate the clouds of darkness, and cause peace to return to our hearts.

—WASHINGTON IRVING

8

Aging Gracefully

With a change in your mindset, aging can look a whole lot different. That wrinkle on your face becomes like the first sentence in a delightful book. Those morning aches and pains become reminders of a life lived to the fullest. A walk outside is all the sweeter for being shorter.

Society has taught us that getting older is something to be feared, but Mother knows best. Listen to her instead. Age with grace, not with worry, and you'll discover how beautiful twilight can be.

You make sacrifices to become a mother, but you really find yourself and your soul.

—MARISKA HARGITAY

My mother, Helen Gould, lived to be almost 101. The last three years of her life were the most productive. She became an avid artist and painted nonstop. She had many art shows in the senior residence in Palm Beach where she resided.

My mother believed that her art would make other residents happier. She would have an art exhibition and allow every friend to take a framed picture to hang in their rooms. Even the doctors and staff chose Helen's paintings. My mom became famous among all the residents.

My mom said to me, "Andy, I tried to make this last chapter of my life memorable and be productive and make people happy to receive a gift. I felt that I had a purpose."

I will never forget my mom who made a difference in so many people's lives. To this day, Helen Gould's art is still exhibited.

—Andrea Stark, friend

The trick is growing up without growing old.

—CASEY STENGEL

One directive was to never leave home without mascara and lipstick, and in my case, she preferred me to wear my contacts not my glasses. You never know who you'll run into.

—Lois J. Cohen, Esq., attorney

Growing old is mandatory. Growing up is optional.

—WALT DISNEY

My mother Helene always possessed wise maternal instincts. An educator by vocation, she seamlessly incorporated her natural teaching techniques and weaved them effortlessly into her mothering style. She made sure all her girls (there are three of us) were raised to have a healthy dose of self-esteem and self-worth.

My mother was not one to offer praise indiscriminately. Instead, she focused on what she felt were our natural strengths and weaknesses. This made her messaging even more impactful because we thoroughly trusted her insights, even when at times we did not want to.

Helene told us there is always going to be someone richer, prettier, and smarter out there. She understood the value in not getting too attached to being the most "whatever" in life. Mother shared a perceptive truth.

Some days, we may feel like a star, enjoying center stage, while other days we might play a more supportive, backseat role. She advised me to embrace both roles with grace and enjoyment. While she shared that it may be fun to be front stage and center, she also knew how important it is to let others star and have their moment to shine as well.

My mother taught me my sense of self-worth must come from an inner knowingness of who I am and not to let other's judgements define or diminish my sense of self-worth or specialness. What a relief to learn that my self-esteem and sense of self must ultimately come from me—

that I must tap into an inner wisdom rather than over relying on the ephemeral opinions of others.

My mother is a great believer that how we make others feel in a room is so much more important than what room we find ourselves in. While always aware of the power of a woman's femininity, she encouraged my sisters and me to enjoy being female. She encouraged body confidence and never made us feel self-conscious about our looks. Helene held the power to make us feel beautiful, smart, and worthy. She strongly encouraged us to set high standards for ourselves, to shoot for our dreams and bloom where we were planted.

Her fundamental words of wisdom are the foundations by which I live my life today. The central principles which help me to embrace myself and encourage others, as I engage in this magical experience called life.

I appreciate my mother every day for being a wise and talented teacher who continues to be my bright light and cherished advisor.

—Dr. Robi Ludwig, friend

Youth fades; love droops; the leaves of friendship fall; a mother's secret hope outlives them all.

—OLIVER WENDELL HOLMES

Keep busy, make your life exciting as you possibly can. You can get older, but don't be old.

—Robin Baker Leacock, filmmaker

Your arms were always open when I needed a hug. Your heart understood when I needed a friend. Your gentle eyes were stern when I needed a lesson. Your strength and love have guided me and given me wings to fly.

—SARAH MALIN

"Always stand up straight—nobody likes a slouchy girl. They're looking because they wish they were as tall and as beautiful as you!" This was my mother's way of making me feel comfortable in my own skin. She said it so many times to me and my older sister that I can almost hear it in my sleep.

—Susan Allan Block, friend

"Stand up straight."

To say that my mother was a stickler for good posture would be an understatement. Good posture was almost a religion for her. Self-confidence, an attractive appearance, good health and more all depended on erect comportment. I've read that Consuelo Vanderbilt's mother forced her to wear a steel brace to make sure her young daughter never deviated from perpendicularity. My own mother was by no means cruel in the way she trained me. But she was vigilant, effective and, I believe, right.

The downside of her instruction was that other girls' mothers would needle their daughters to stand up straight like me.

To promote proper carriage, my mother enrolled me in dance classes. As I grew taller and more in danger of stooping to meet the world at eye level, these classes took on extra urgency.

As a result of all those lessons and leotards, I remain an ardent audience member and patron of dance. In fact, I am currently Executive Producer of the young company Tabula Rasa Dance Theater.

My mother, now 90, still stands straight. I expect to at that age as well. Good posture gives us, or so she continues to tell me, presence.

—Amy Fine Collins, Executive Producer of Tabula Rasa Dance Theater

The days are long but the years are short.

—GRETCHEN RUBIN

"Just because it's old doesn't mean you have to throw it away," my mother said. And so, I inherited boxes of *Elite Styles Magazine* from the early 20th century, as well as Herman Miller wooden chairs from my father's office. And ornate gold rimmed frames with Burliuk and Neysmyth and William Henry Howe dark and dreary paintings.

—Dede Gotthelf, hotelier

I owe so much to my mother. It was her wisdom and guidance that shaped my individuality and unique sense of style, leading by example with her eclectic Bohemian fashionista aesthetic and her urging me to always be myself.

It was through this that I was voted class individualist in high school. Borrowing from poet Robert Frost, she would always say: "When you come to a fork in the road, study the footprints and take the road less traveled."

And we sure did a lot of traveling. She took me around the world on shopping trips, always searching for a touch of vintage alongside the latest designer labels.

One time, she came to my high school in a netted Schiaparelli hat with birds and flowers stacked with Bakelite brackets. She was truly an Uptown kind of lady who was well known at emporiums like Barney's and Bergdorf Goodman. Staff was always eager to be of service as soon as she walked through the doors.

My mother would always say that no matter what you are wearing, you must have great shoes and a bag to complete the look. I have followed that mantra to this very day. In fact, my mother's style wisdom came from her mother, so this same code of ethics in fashion has been passed down through the generations. I am instilling it in my daughter too, who already has a penchant for good shoes and bags—even when wearing sweats!

Now as a shoe and fashion designer, I am taking this family knowledge and making a business of it. And being an individualist thanks to my mother, my designs zig when the others zag. Meanwhile, as a businesswoman, I'm always speaking the truth. In fact, some may say I'm too honest—but at least everyone knows where they stand when dealing with my mother's daughter!

—Tracy Stern, fashion designer

No matter how old a mother is, she watches her middle-aged children for signs of improvement.

—FLORIDA SCOTT-MAXWELL

My mother is 96 years of age and resides in Los Angeles, where I recently visited her. It was a bittersweet visit and departure, knowing that there is always a strong possibility that my last visit could be the last I see her. Her heart is slowing down and her memory is beginning to fail her; thus, the memories are more present.

I would like to say that my best qualities are attributed to my mother, Rosa Elvia Portillo De Iraheta. Where do I begin to pay tribute to a woman that taught me what unconditional love is. How to be a proper lady and have the proper manners, and how to be kind and loving towards others and to always look at the bright side of things and the best in others.

As a child, I learned that giving was more exciting and fulfilling than receiving. I vividly remember the numerous times when my mother would receive a compliment on a brooch or any other piece of jewelry and the very next day, she would have the item gift-wrapped and delivered to the person that had complimented her. It was such a wonderful and kind gesture that is so engrained in me that to this day I can picture the joy expressed on my mother's face—her great big smile when she would get a visit or phone call from the individual to thank her for her gesture.

Today, I call these memories random acts of kindness, and brooches are one of my favorite jewelry pieces.

—Ellie Johnson, friend

9
Everlasting Love

True love never fades. The dedication your mother gave you from the moment you are born is pure. It is unselfish. It is meant to be.

She was destined to be your precious mother. You were created for her. The magical bond will never fade and only grows stronger with time. Paul McCartney of The Beatles beautifully summed it up when he sang the lyrics, "And in the end the love you take is equal to the love you make."

No one in your life will ever love you as your mother does. There is no love as pure, unconditional, and strong as a mother's love.

—CHRISTIANE NORTHRUP

"Never put off until tomorrow what you can do today." In other words, time is of the essence, use it wisely. This is my advice to my son Leo.

—Emma-Jane McCormack, friend

A mother's arms are more comforting than anyone else's.

—DIANA, PRINCESS OF WALES

My mother's wisest life lesson came from her death. But it's not about death. It's about life. And how to live it. Even when it comes time to give it up. There are fates worse than death.

—Katharine Sands, literary agent

If you want your children to be intelligent, read them fairy tales. If you want them to be more intelligent, read them more fairy tales.

—ALBERT EINSTEIN

My mother has always been my inspiration and my guardian angel. Without her eternal guidance, I would be lost. She is fearless!

—Carmen D'Alessio, nightlife impresario

When you look into your mother's eyes, you know that is the purest love you can find on this earth.

—MITCH ALBOM

My mother was a tower of strength, love, integrity, and kindness. One piece of advice that I constantly refer to, particularly when making meaningful decisions about my overall life is, "You can't take anything with you from this world, but what you leave behind is priceless."

—Cassandra Seidenfeld, friend

Mother's love is peace. It need not be acquired, it need not be deserved.

—ERICH FROMM

I was with my mother on the day she had a major stroke. Just minutes before she said the following: "The secret to a happy life is knowing how to make your own self happy. You can't rely on others. No one knows better than you on what brings you happiness."

These were the last words she said to me before she had a stroke and was rushed to the hospital. She passed away just two days later without uttering another word. My mother was Ruth Brenniser.

—Sandra Familet, friend

You may lose everything in this world, and a mother's love will alone stick by you; you may go down, down to the lowest depths of degradation, be steeped in crime and sin, an outcast from your fellow beings, when, at the eleventh hour, the memory of your mother and her undying love may come like a golden cloud, and with all its early strength and warmth, may be the means of wresting you from the very jaws of hell.

—T. AUGUSTUS FORBES LEITH

In Yiddish, "Ales Ba Einem, Iz Nishdo Ba Keinem."

Translated, it means, "Everything by one person doesn't exist by no one."

That was my late mother Yafa Zur advising me regarding finding my one and only. She genuinely meant, 'Mira, learn to compromise.' However, being me, I had a different way to translate it.

"If I cannot find all in one, I'll combine a few to make that one whole."

—Mira Tzur, actress

No matter how old you are, you always want your mother's love and acceptance.

—HILARY GROSSMAN

My beautiful Hungarian mother, Marion Gold, may have been a bit more Zsa Zsa Gabor than Julia Child in the kitchen, yet nonetheless was a wonderful cook who made meatloaf in the shape of a heart. Several weeks after her 80th birthday, she lay on her deathbed in her apartment in Queens, struggling to breathe from pulmonary hypertension, but held me in her loving gaze and spoke with her own brand of wisdom—a recipe, really, of how to live life without her.

"Love and care will make everything all right. Look deep inside your heart and you will find the answer. Have more faith in life." And then a final endearment of, "Have fun." Hastily jotted on a slip of pale blue paper are her words, tucked into my wallet, dated October 17, 2006, and guiding me still.

—Rozanne Gold, chef and writer

A mother's love for her child is like nothing else in the world. It knows no law, no pity, it dares all things and crushes down remorselessly all that stands in its path.

—AGATHA CHRISTIE

All women become like their mothers. That is their tragedy. No man does. That's his.

—OSCAR WILDE, *The Importance of Being Earnest*

We have a secret in our culture, and it's not that birth is painful. It's that women are strong.

—LAURA STAVOE HARM

Mothers were the same all through the centuries, a great sisterhood of love and service, the remembered and the unremembered alike.

—L. M. MONTGOMERY,
Anne of Ingleside

My Mother's Words of Wisdom

Words exchanged between daughters
and mothers—in the moment or in
memory—can carry enormous weight.

—Deborah Tannen

The stories shared by the many people who made this collection possible highlight the incredible value of a mother's love, attention and advice. To this, I wanted to add some of the lessons my own mother taught me growing up, which together have helped me become the person I am today.

Mother Knows Best

There will never be anyone like your mother. Cherish her.

• • •

In life, you can only rely on yourself.

• • •

Do good and forget about it. Do bad and worry about it. Always try to do good.

• • •

It's all in your mind. Mind over matter.

• • •

If you want something, earn it. Don't spend it until you have earned it.

• • •

You have heard the old wives' tale, "You are lucky if you have enough real friends to count on the fingers of one hand." Yes, it is true.

• • •

You only have one name.
Do not ruin your reputation.

• • •

Do not air your dirty laundry.
A family has to stick together.

• • •

A man should always be a
gentleman and a lady, a lady.

• • •

Don't let anyone push you around.
No one is any better than you.

• • •

Before you pass judgement, ignore.

• • •

Do not gossip.

• • •

Penny wise, pound foolish.

• • •

If you have children, be prepared
to look after them.

• • •

Never comment on physical appearance.
We are all different and all can change.

• • •

Don't feel sorry for yourself.
Do not put yourself down.

• • •

After all, tomorrow is another day.

Simple Advice

Always look your best. Dress appropriately for the occasion. Look your best, no matter your budget.

• • •

Seize the opportunity.

• • •

Don't be a follower. Be a leader.

• • •

Do not discuss money, politics, religion or family business.

• • •

Walk a lot. It clears your mind
as well as gives you activity.

• • •

No time for phonies. Invest your energy
in the people that really matter.

• • •

Read. Being well-read is being
well-equipped for life.

• • •

Go to church for God, not the priest.
My mother always said that if you have faith
and walk with God you can handle anything.

• • •

Get over it. Get over yourself.

• • •

Stay real. You should have your self-respect.

• • •

An education is important.

• • •

You should always look after
the cook and the cashier.

• • •

No matter your budget, always spend money
on good food rather than the furniture.

• • •

Get a job, save your money.

• • •

Keep one eye open in any situation.

• • •

Never ASSume. It makes an
ass out of you and me.

• • •

Age is only a number; you do
not need to keep count.

• • •

If you do not like something, do something about it. If you want help, look at the end of your arms.

• • •

When married, share everything but keep a little independence.

• • •

Live and let live.

• • •

Laugh loud and often.

Rules to Live By

Respect your parents.

• • •

Eat healthy with plenty of vegetables and fruit.

• • •

Drink lots of water.

• • •

Look after yourself—teeth, nails and hair are so important.

• • •

Do not do drugs nor smoke.

• • •

Manners are important. Always say please and thank you. With good manners, you can go anywhere.

• • •

Treat everyone as you would like to be treated. Treat people on the way up as you would want to be treated on the way down.

• • •

If you have nothing good to say, do not say anything.

• • •

Always be kind. Do not waste energy on negativity.

• • •

Don't be selfish.

• • •

Have faith. With that, you can do anything.

• • •

Save your money.

• • •

Live every day like it is your last.

Conclusion

> My mother...she is beautiful, softened at the edges and tempered with a spine of steel. I want to grow old and be like her.
>
> —Jodi Picoult

I HOPE THIS BOOK has brought you closer to your Mother. By sharing these stories, it celebrates their lives. And for those of you whose mothers have passed and you think they are no longer with us: With their shared memories and words, hearing their voices in your heads, making their favorite foods, purchasing their favorite flowers...they're still here.

Mothers have a unique ability to shape our identities, nurture our growth, and guide us towards our full potential. With their unconditional love, unwavering support, and selfless devotion, they help us navigate life's challenges and emerge stronger, wiser, and more compassionate individuals. May this book serve as a testament to the enduring wisdom, grace, and love that mothers bring to our world, and may it inspire future generations to cherish and honor these remarkable women who give so much of themselves to us.

Acknowledgments

A few years ago, I sent out a simple email to family, friends and clients asking for their mothers' wisdom. My sincere thanks to those who responded and contributed to this book.

The team at Hatherleigh Press for their patience.

The Lawlor Media Group Team.

Dr Jeffrey Bradford; I could not have done it without you.

To all my friends in the media; thank you for your continued support.

To all my friends and clients who didn't give a quote; there is always the next book.

All our mothers and mothers-in-law.

And of course all the fathers, without whom we would not be here.

About the Author

Norah Lawlor began her career in Canada hosting a cable TV show and producing fashion shows, bringing the hottest Canadian talent to New York. This fired her ambitions to build her career in Communications and PR and after moving to New York City she initially handled Events and PR for the nightlife scene from which her success evolved into the launch of Lawlor Media Group, Inc.

The Agency, in business for over 25 years, has an innovative approach to generating buzz and media interest for her clientele, which includes names familiar to the New York, Hamptons and Palm Beach, in the social and society scene.

Today, Norah's business has metamorphosized, providing strategic PR consulting, communications and campaign implementation for a roster of national and International luxury lifestyle brands and clients encompassing real estate, charitable organizations, fashion, travel, health & beauty, hospitality, television, movie premieres, authors plus celebrities and high-profile personalities.